John Dury Geden

The Doctrine of a future Life

As contained in the Old Testament Scripture

John Dury Geden

The Doctrine of a future Life
As contained in the Old Testament Scripture

ISBN/EAN: 9783337060879

Printed in Europe, USA, Canada, Australia, Japan

Cover: Foto ©ninafisch / pixelio.de

More available books at **www.hansebooks.com**

THE DOCTRINE OF A FUTURE LIFE

AS CONTAINED IN

THE OLD TESTAMENT SCRIPTURES.

𝔄 Discourse,

DELIVERED IN WESLEY CHAPEL, CAMBORNE,

July 28th, 1874,

IN CONNECTION WITH THE ASSEMBLING OF THE

WESLEYAN-METHODIST CONFERENCE.

BEING

THE FIFTH LECTURE ON THE FOUNDATION OF THE

LATE JOHN FERNLEY, ESQ.

BY JOHN DURY GEDEN,

TUTOR IN HEBREW AND CLASSICS, DIDSBURY COLLEGE, MANCHESTER.

LONDON :

WESLEYAN CONFERENCE OFFICE,

2, CASTLE-STREET, CITY-ROAD ;

SOLD AT 66, PATERNOSTER-ROW.

1874.

ON THE DOCTRINE OF A FUTURE LIFE AS CONTAINED IN THE OLD TESTAMENT SCRIPTURES.

THE aim of the present inquiry is to determine how far the doctrine of a Future Life is contained in the Old Testament, and to state in brief what that doctrine is. A larger, loftier topic, one more sacred and heart-stirring, in certain respects one more difficult, could hardly occupy us. History, philosophy, science, all have a substantive interest in the question; while for the disciple of Christ, bearing, as it does, directly upon the grounds, the matter, and the sanctions of his faith, it cannot but possess an unspeakable gravity and attractiveness. At the present moment, likewise, the importance attaching to our thesis by its very nature is indefinitely heightened by the keen public feeling which gathers around all Scripture dogma; by the ruthless and often arbitrary criticism, which menaces the ancient glory of the earlier canon of Holy Writ; and, in particular, by the general agreement and positive assertion, on the part of the contemporary Biblical scepticism, that the Old Testament either does not contain the doctrine of a Future Life at all, or that that doctrine is only found there under pitiful proportions, and with infinite haziness and uncertainty of outline.

I.

Against those who take the position now indicated, we maintain, to begin with, that the Old Testament carries on

V.   B

the very face of it the doctrine of a Life to Come, and that, within certain limits, the doctrine is marked by sharply drawn and easily distinguishable features. We should be quite content to stake this issue upon the judgment of any man of ordinary sense and candour, who should read the documents for the first time, apart from all bias, simply as matter of curiosity, and for purposes of information and knowledge. What would such a person find in the Old Testament, so far as our subject is concerned? No doubt he would encounter a number of passages—such passages, however, being really much fewer than is sometimes supposed—which seem to affirm distinctly enough, that human existence ends with the present life. He would hear the plaintive voice of Job contrasting the felled tree with the dead man, how the one might spring again, if it only scented the vivifying water; but the other—where is he, when he giveth up the ghost? "As the waters fail from the sea, and the flood decayeth and drieth up : so man lieth down, and riseth not : till the heavens be no more, they shall not awake, nor be raised out of their sleep" (Job xiv. 7—12). The wise woman of Tekoah would stand in his presence before the great king of Israel, and her words would pass unchallenged : "For we must needs die, and are as water spilt on the ground, which cannot be gathered up again" (2 Samuel xiv. 14). Either David, or a fellow-psalmist, would pray in his hearing : "O spare me, that I may recover strength, before I go hence, and be no more !" (Psalm xxxix. 13.) Or, taking up his similitude, he would say : "As for man, his days are as grass : as a flower of the field, so he flourisheth. For the wind passeth over it, and it is gone ; and the place thereof shall know it no more" (Psalm ciii. 15, 16). Or, speaking to God, the holy singer would ask—" Wilt Thou show wonders to the dead? shall the dead arise and praise thee?" (Psalm lxxxviii. 10): then, answering his own question, he would aver, that the son of man is nothing, for " his breath goeth forth, he returneth to his earth ; in that very day his thoughts perish " (Psalm cxlvi. 3, 4). So, in Isaiah, the stricken Hezekiah would be seen pleading with God for life on the ground that death and the grave could not celebrate him, neither could they that go down to the pit have hope in his truth (Isaiah xxxviii. 18). To crown all, the dirgelike tones of Koheleth, " the Preacher," bemoaning his kind, would strike upon his ear : " For that which befalleth the sons of men befalleth beasts ; even one thing befalleth them : as the one dieth, so dieth the other ; yea, they have all one breath ; so that a man hath no preeminence above a beast " (Ecclesiastes iii. 19) : or, as the same sad oracle elsewhere utters it with dogmatic emphasis : " The dead know not any thing, neither have they any more a reward ; . . . for there is no work, nor device, nor knowledge, nor wisdom, in the grave, whither thou goest " (Ecclesiastes ix. 5—10).

All this, and more to the same effect, our stranger would light upon in reading the Hebrew Scriptures ; but he would quite as frequently meet with other and very different doctrine. In the midst of a genealogical table of patriarchs he would be startled with the record, that one of their number did not die like the rest, but disappeared from the earth, God taking him because of his exemplary piety (Genesis v. 24). The night before the fatal battle at Gilboa he would find himself shut in with Saul and the Witch of Endor, and would hear the dead Samuel tell the fainting monarch, how he and his sons next day would be slain, and be with him (1 Samuel xxviii. 15—19). Long after this he would go up with Elijah into the bedchamber at Zarephath, and would listen to the rugged prophet's prayer : " O Lord my God, . . . let this child's soul come into him again!'" (1 Kings xvii. 21.) And beyond the range of the historic books, he would mark how his Volume teaches, that the spirit of man, when he dies, returns to God who gave it (Ecclesiastes xii. 7); that wicked men pass by like a whirlwind, while the righteous abideth for ever (Proverbs x. 25); that in another world God will judge both the righteous and the wicked (Ecclesiastes iii. 17, xi. 9); and that the dead, small and great, shall finally appear before the Divine tribunal for judgment (Daniel vii. 10, xii. 2). In other words, the Old Testament would be seen to carry with it, as one of its most patent and obvious teachings, the doctrine that man lives after he is dead, and that the present world is not the limit of existence for its human inhabitants. Our reader might as well doubt whether the Vêda teaches the worship of the sky and of fire, or the Zendavesta the dogma of the resurrection, or the Confucian Classics the obligation of filial piety, as whether a Future Life is taught by the Law, the Prophets, and the Psalms.

How he would interpret the apparently conflicting voices of his Volume on the subject in question, is another point; and this would be determined very much by his personal character, and by the view which he took of the circumstances, aims, and moral qualifications of its writers. If he were a man of detail, who must bring everything under the microscope; or a one-sided man, always missing the half at least of whatever object met his intellectual eye; or a man to whom prose and poetry, plain language and figure, were all one; or, again, a man having no moral susceptibilities, and no capacity of appreciating moral evidence; he would probably conclude that, with regard to the doctrine of a Future Life, the documents were a jumble of inconsistencies, the authors saying and unsaying almost in the same breath, and that, on the whole, it was difficult to decide which way the balance of their collective witness tended. Such would very likely be the finding of the atom-searching, unequally developed, pragmatical, and purely scientific mind.

But suppose the documents to have fallen into better hands. Let our reader irresistibly take the impression, which countless minds of the nobler sort have actually taken, that, diverse as these writings were, they had a marvellous unity of spirit, substance, and scope; that their authors were clearly men of commanding intelligence and of transcendent moral worth; and that there was an air and a tone, belonging alike to them and to their compositions, which bespoke a preternatural afflatus and guidance. Suppose him to be thus impressed. Suppose him further to be well able to discern between categorical statement, and the many-coloured vestures of imagination and fancy; between the formal dialect of science and the free speech of the multitude. Withal let his intellectual constitution and habit oblige him to examine every subject under diversified lights; and while he is not disregardful of detail, let him know how to sweep a large and comprehensive field of thought. The conclusion arrived at by a man of this description would differ widely from that of the person with whom he is put in contrast. We do not say that he would pronounce at once, that his Book gives forth a single and absolutely certain sound in relation to a Future Existence. He might think that here and there the voice was stammering and muffled; and he could scarcely fail to note that its utterances were clearer and more frequent in the later than in the earlier portions of the Volume. But he would not feel it necessary to press Oriental language to its uttermost literalities. He would not, in the name of scientific truth, compel ancient chroniclers and bards to wear the iron fetters of algebra. He would not make it matter of conscience to find disagreements everywhere and correspondences nowhere. He would comprehend that most of the passages, which seem to speak of death as annihilation, are to be understood of the complete and final extinction, which man then suffers relatively to the present world; that this is the obvious meaning of the passages; and that it would be pedantry and sciolism to expound them in any other way. Indeed, we do not hesitate to say, that such a reader of Old Testament Scripture, as is here supposed, would in all likelihood perceive, that while his authors unequivocally teach the doctrine of a Future Life—a doctrine, too, having strongly-pronounced and most impressive characteristics—there is really no instance in their writings of seemingly incongruous teaching, which does not admit of easy explanation; and that, considering the style and quality of the Book, its view of a Hereafter ought to be regarded as consistent, homogeneous, and one.

II.

Here, however, we part with our stranger reader, and take a different position. Assuming that the Old Testament contains the doctrine of a Life to Come, we sit us down with the scholar, philosopher, theologian, and critic, and seek to trace and define the doctrine, neither omitting anything of consequence which certainly belongs to it, nor importing anything from without which is extraneous or doubtful. In attempting this, we do not shut ourselves up to the documents alone, to the exclusion of all other lights, any more than we should do this in studying Herodotus or Pindar, Thucydides or Aristotle. Many and various considerations may come in aid of our inquiries, checking, correcting, guiding, determining them. History, language, tradition, the mythologies or theosophies of Babylonia, Persia, and

Egypt—these and other witnesses may be appealed to where the way is dark, and illumination is desirable. All that learning and honest reasoning can bring to enlighten us may be cordially welcomed. Only we must never cease for the time to be scientific students, having a definite object in view, of a series of Hebrew and Aramæan documents, dating through a period which ranges from some fifteen or sixteen hundred to some three or four hundred years before the Christian era.

In speaking thus, we do not confound things which differ. We shall pay no homage to the professed sceptic. He is commonly the smallest and most self-sufficient of mankind; and we are as little careful to satisfy his sentimental doubts, as we are disposed to recognize his principles, or adopt his methods. Neither do we accept—on the contrary, we utterly disallow and repudiate—a number of conclusions, touching the origin, constitution, and character of certain books of the Old Testament, at which the Biblical critics of the so-called advanced school claim to have arrived, and which, as they declare, the ignorant, the prejudiced, and the interested alone can scruple.

For example, according to the critics in question, the books of Moses are a blundering patchwork of fragments taken from different sources, and seamed together by various hands, at times long posterior to the Mosaic epoch; the book of Deuteronomy, in particular, being clearly " written not long before the Babylonish captivity." * The last twenty-seven chapters of the prophecy of Isaiah, again, are no work, it is affirmed, of the mind and pen which produced the first thirty-nine chapters; they are the composition of an unknown author—call him the Pseudo- or Deutero-Isaiah,

---

* Colenso's "Lectures on the Pentateuch and the Moabite Stone." Preface, p. vii.

if you please—who lived long after the son of Amoz was gone to his fathers. In like manner, the Book of Daniel— our oracles pronounce—though commonly assumed to be a record dating from the era of the Babylonian Nebuchadnezzar and Belshazzar, was in reality composed three hundred years later, in the days of Antiochus Epiphanes; and this alleged fact is signalised as "one of the highest triumphs . . . of the more recent criticism." *

Now we contend that the literary dogmas here cited, and they are but types of a class, are not established on evidence. Their parentage is historically and logically traceable to foregone conclusions respecting miracle, prophecy, and other supernatural elements of the Old Testament Volume. They are the handiwork of as perverse and Procrustean an ingenuity as ever, consciously or unconsciously, tortured truth into fable since the world began. They fly in the face of all reason and analogy. They are arbitrary, inconsistent, pedantic, and absurd. The well-known Jehovist and Elohist theory, as it has often been applied to explain the structure of the Pentateuch, and other books of Hebrew Scripture, we hold to be a whimsical illusion, which after-ages will chronicle among the literary portents of this nineteenth Christian century. If anything is certain—by the concurrent evidence of matter and manner, of genius and form, of tradition and history, this is certain : that the writings which pass under the name of Moses—the fifth section of them quite as much as the other four—are the work, in the main, of a single author; that that author was Moses himself; that the other Old Testament books presuppose the Pentateuch, and are built upon it; and that, in point of fact, the Roll of the Law, as Moses left it, became, to compare great things with small, what the Koran in after-times became to Moham-

* Quotation in Dr. Pusey's " Lectures on Daniel." Preface, p. vi.

medanism, a historical, doctrinal, and linguistic basis for the whole body of the subsequent literature of Israel. With respect to the grand Messianic paragraph of Isaiah, and its alleged composition by some great Unknown of later date, we might very well object, that this is hardly more conceivable than if an English poet of the present day, none knowing anything as to his name, or pedigree, or dwelling-place, should add another half to our Shakespeare, in quality the perfect equal of his Tempest, Hamlet, or King Lear. But we let this pass. The truth is, that if the closing chapters of Isaiah are what Ewald and his school allege, that most lofty, tender, plaintive, captivating, solemn, and awfully religious composition, written in the very name of the God of truth, and again and again making Him to stake His natural and moral attributes upon its contents, becomes a stupendous forgery, the like of which does not darken the annals of literary fraud—the nearest approach to it, perhaps, being found in the Book of Daniel, if that also is the late production which the German critics and their English acolytes so confidently declare it to be.

We do not affirm that the writer of the Pentateuch made no use of preexisting documents. Neither do we pledge ourselves that no explanatory additions were incorporated with the early historic texts of the Old Testament by later and anonymous hands. Still less do we deny the incontrovertible fact, that, despite the jealousy which watched over the documents, they have suffered, less or more, like the sacred writings of the New Testament, from ignorance, mistake, and other accidents. But granting all this, and not only admitting, but even courting serious, reasonable criticism, we hold that the popular judgment respecting the authorship, the relative age, the historic truth, and the substantial genuineness of the Hebrew Scriptures, has the endorsement of the highest science upon it: and on this platform we purpose attempting to track the Old Testament doctrine of a Future Life down the line of the Records, beginning from the remotest periods to which the Mosaic narrative conducts us, and descending to the time when the last Israelitish prophet bids farewell to the scene of his evangelistic ministry.

I. In the carrying out of our programme, we have naturally to do, first, with that mysterious and unique period of human history, commencing with the birth of our race, and extending to the epoch of Moses and the exodus of Israel from Egypt. And here, taking into account at once the length of time covered by the narrative, the prefatory character of the earlier half of it, and the narrow limits of space to which the historian confines himself, we need not wonder if little is said on the subject of the Future Life. And, as matter of fact, there is no direct statement of the doctrine. Nevertheless it would be passing strange if a book, avowedly designed to show in what way God dealt with man from the beginning as a being capable of religion, should be wholly silent respecting the ultimate, and therefore the most solemn sanction of all moral agency. Such, however, is not the case. Our doctrine is implied in the language used by Moses, on the very first page of his history, to describe the original constitution and circumstances of mankind. A creature formed in the image and after the likeness of the Eternal and Invisible God; possessed of a spiritual essence, by its origin and qualities indefinitely lifting him above the rest of the animal creation; holding personal intercourse with the manifested Deity; laid under sacred charge of fidelity to the gift of life that was in him; a creature so represented is virtually affirmed, as the all but inspired Book of " Wisdom " has it, to have been made for incorruption; and, by the necessity of things, he must himself have been aware that this was his sublime prerogative and destiny. Uncivilized in the common acceptation of the term, primeval man may have been; but, by his very nature, he cannot have been ignorant, that he belonged to the sphere of the heavenly not the mundane; that his closest affinities were with God and spiritual beings, not with the brute; that the everlasting was his province and goal, not the temporary; that, in fact, either on earth or elsewhere, he was heir to an existence coeval with the life of the Immortal One, whose child he was. The terms employed to describe man's moral position after his offence—" And now, lest he put forth his hand, and take also of the tree of life, . . . and live for ever "—make it absolutely certain, that in sinning he had forfeited, and that he himself knew quite well that he had forfeited, the immortality which was his birthright.

How men's religious intelligence and moral dignity sank with the Fall the historic record sufficiently suggests, and no darker picture of spiritual depravation is possible than that which Moses draws in depicting the condition of mankind before the flood (Genesis vi. 5). But the antediluvians were not the evildoers they were, because they knew nothing of an unseen world, and of another state of existence. The fact that the holy " Enoch was not," was in all probability at once a startling reminder of invisible realities already familiar to them, and a gracious disclosure of these realities under a new and most impressive form. And apart from all speculation, and shutting out entirely the reflex light of later Scripture, Moses, in the brief but pregnant passage now referred to, must be held to teach unequivocally, that some few years only before the second birth of the world on the mountains of Ararat mankind were owners of the awful paradox, that not to be, for the good at least, is still to be—with God.

We think we might argue substantially the same doctrine from the terms in which God communicated with Noah after the deluge, touching the matter of guilty homicide : " Whoso sheddeth man's blood, by man shall his blood be shed : for in the image of God made he man " (Genesis ix. 6). What adequate meaning can these words afford if they do not involve that same idea of the immaterial, supramundane, and immortal nature of man, which we found contained in the language used to describe his original formation and estate ? To explain them as though a murderer must die because his victim walks erect, or is, by force of intellect, the master of the panther and the wolf, is as distinct a lilliputianism as a creeping exegesis ever fell into. By implication this Divine ordinance of capital punishment for murder was a solemn announcement, first to the generation which received it, then to all after-generations, that the soul of man lives after the body is dead.

Once more, at a much later stage of the pre-Mosaic period, we find clear traces of the knowledge of a Future Life in a significant formula relating to death, which, with slight variations, appears again and again in the Book of Genesis. " Thou shalt go to thy fathers in peace," said God to Abram, in that wonderful apocalypse at the Hebron oak-grove (Genesis xv. 15); and, accordingly, Abraham " gave up the ghost . . . in a good old age . . . and was gathered to his people " (Genesis xxv. 8). In like manner Ishmael " gave up the ghost, and . . . was gathered unto his people " (Genesis xxv. 17). Precisely the same language is employed concerning Isaac when he died (Genesis xxxv. 29). And so of Jacob it is said, that having commanded his sons, he " yielded up the ghost, and was gathered unto his people "

(Genesis xlix. 33). Now these terms, the substantial equivalence of which we assume, are not simply a periphrasis for death. For though death is, no doubt, part of the meaning of the expression "go to thy fathers," which occurs in the first of our passages, wherever the other expression— to be gathered to one's people—is found, an explicit line is drawn between it and death. Abraham, Ishmael, Isaac, Jacob, all "died," *and* were "gathered to their people." As little can the words be understood of the act of burial, for in every instance quoted, save one, the dead man is represented as "going to his fathers," and as "gathered to his people," before he is buried. By parity of reason, the expressions cannot be used of the state of the body as laid in the same grave with its ancestors. Besides, Abraham at least, who was to "go to his fathers," and was actually "gathered to his people," did not lie with his Mesopotamian relatives, being entombed as a stranger in the strange land in which he lived and died. And to expound the terms as though they meant merely becoming, in relation to this world, what all who die must of necessity become, is to make Moses say, that when the patriarchs died they were dead—a view of his words altogether intolerable, except for critics, who deem him the literary weakling which every page of his writings testifies he was not. No. Whatever secondary value may belong to the language in question, this at least lies at the root of it, that while a great gulf parts the dead and the living, Sheol—as the Pentateuch calls it—the realm of the dead, is also a realm of life, and that when man dies, he goes to the ever-multiplying congregation and fellowship of his nearer or remoter kindred in the unseen world. Thus, without pressing dubious passages, the opening pages of the Old Testament are seen to teach the doctrine of a Life to Come; and in perfect harmony with all we know of the primeval faiths of our race—the Babylonian and Assyrian, for example—from other and less certain sources, men, both within and beyond the Shemitic stock of peoples, are represented by Moses as, centuries before his own era, holding this doctrine, and framing their current speech under its influence. What the precise dimension or quality of their knowledge was, we have no means of ascertaining. This would greatly depend on the degree of their enlightenment as to the character and moral government of God. Where these fundamental religious verities were clearly apprehended, the notions of the separate state of the soul, of Divine retribution, and of immortality, may have been much more distinct and luminous than we sometimes imagine.

II. The section of the Old Testament next claiming our thought is that which records the deliverance of Israel from Egypt under Moses, and their eventual settlement in Canaan, together with the founding and early history of that venerable system of theology and jurisprudence, known as the Mosaic Institute. In other words, we are now to consider what the Books of Exodus, Leviticus, Numbers, Deuteronomy, and Joshua have to say on the subject of our inquiry.

And here we need not hesitate at once to confess to a feeling of wonder, that the utterances of our documents are so faint and scattered. Considering in how solemn a manner God adopted the seed of Abraham, in the line of Isaac and Jacob, to the estate of national sonship to Himself; considering, likewise, the essential theocratic character of the legislation and economy of Moses; considering, further, that the avowed object, both of the adoption and of the theocracy, was the sanctification of Israel for their own good and that of mankind at large; it is undeniably strange that the supreme sanctions of religion come so little into the fore-

ground, and, so far as we remember, never once present
themselves as matter of express dogmatic teaching. The
absence of all allusion to them in the awful comminations
of Leviticus xxvi. and Deuteronomy xxix. is peculiarly
notable, and can only be explained upon the principle, that
it was not the will of God that a Future Life should be
urged by Moses as a formal and prominent sanction of
obedience to His laws. This feature of the Mosaic legislation,
it is well known, was made by a distinguished prelate of the
English Church, the basis of a masterly argument for the
" Divine Legation of Moses," the contention being that a
lawgiver, who, without appealing to a Future Life, could
stake the credit of his code upon a Providence which should,
alike for the nation and the individual, in this present world,
through all time, enforce the authority of the code by certain
specified forms of good and evil, must of necessity have
spoken under supernatural inspiration. An unassailable
position, truly, this of Warburton's, if only we allow his
fundamental doctrine in all the length and breadth of it. But
here we hesitate. If Moses did not call the Future World
expressly to his aid, was not his legislation such, in kind
and circumstance, as to suggest throughout, that, behind and
beyond whatever Providential blessing or curse he spoke of,
there lay an inexpressibly greater recompense of reward, the
subject of which was to be the individual human soul, while
an unseen and eternal world should constitute the theatre of
its operation ? Arguing from the nature of the case, we find
ourselves compelled to regard his institutions in this light.
In the first place, to say nothing of Moses himself, the whole
body of the Israelitish people, at the time of the Exodus,
must have been perfectly conversant with the dogmas of the
immortality of the soul, and a Future Life of retribution.
However much opinions may differ as to the date of the

Exode, or as to the race or dynasty of the Egyptian kings under whom Israel was in bondage, or even as to the precise locality of Goshen; no possible assumption is more to be relied upon than this. From the earliest periods of the history of Egypt, all through the course of that history, whatever changes, political or other, the country may have undergone, innumerable native records—monumental, pictorial, and literary—agree to testify, not only that the Egyptians were all and always, so far as we can gather, addicted to the worship of gods many and lords many, but that the doctrines above-named held a conspicuous place in their theology, in their conventional religious symbolism, and in the habit of their domestic, social, and public life. They believed that, when men died, their souls, in the unseen state, were subject to a solemn scrutiny before the bar of God, and according as they proved worthy or wanting, when weighed in the balances of eternal truth, they were adjudged to degradation and misery, or to happiness and honour. The famous *Book of the Dead*, so called, dating, in its most ancient texts, some centuries earlier, ·as is supposed, than the birth of Moses, teems with proof of the general acceptance of such a faith among the Egyptians. Indeed, to this day, one of the objects which most commonly meet the eye of the traveller in the lower Nile valley, and with which Egyptologers at home become soonest acquainted in the prosecution of their studies, is the sculptured or painted representation, under different forms, on temple walls, on sarcophagi, in papyrus rolls, and otherwise, of the judgment scene of the *Amenti*, or Hades, with its dread assemblage of divinities and genii, its simple yet striking apparatus of holy trial, and its suggestive symbols of doom. And allowing all possible weight to the consideration, that difference of race, comparative geographical isolation, and a chasm of social inequality, may have shut the Israelites out, to some extent, from the sphere of Egyptian thought and life, it is incredible, considering their long residence in Egypt, and the closeness of the contact into which we know them to have come with their Egyptian masters, but that the idea of the Future Life must have wrought itself into the very texture of their being. Indeed, the Mosaic history and legislation both make it only too clear, that the religious sentiments and practices of Egypt had taken a firm hold upon Israel.

Now, this being so, the teaching and precepts of the law-giver, backed as they were by the miracles of the Exodus and the Wilderness, can have had no surer effect than to purge, and to render more vivid and intense, the views of the Israelites on the subject of the invisible state and its realities. To their minds, apart from the traditions of their race, the doctrine of the world to come was inseparably linked with faith in an omniscient, just, and mighty God, and with the peremptory obligations of moral rectitude. Indeed, it was this faith, together with the energy of con-science naturally springing from and attending it, which determined, to a great degree, the opinions alike of the Egyptians and of Israel with respect to the Future Life. Whatever, therefore, served to elevate, to the mind and heart of the Israelites, their conception of God, and to quicken and sustain their moral tone, would react upon their thoughts concerning a Hereafter, and if not formally, yet really and in truth, would be to them a new revelation of coming destiny. And if this be granted, what could more certainly conduct to such an issue than those awful manifestations of the power, goodness, and purity of Jehovah, which addressed themselves to their corporeal sense, together with those scarcely less awful views of the Divine holiness—views, let us say in passing, which are absolutely unique, and have

V. C

no parallel whatever, in the religious literature of mankind
—conveyed by the theological instructions, the ceremonial
ordinances, and the moral precepts of the Mosaic law? With
Sinai in sight, and with all that significant array of Divinely
appointed symbols—the tabernacle, the priesthood, the
sacrifices—continually in their presence, every one telling
with manifold tongues of the infinite sanctity of God, and of
the need of a corresponding sanctity in man, what necessity
was there that Moses should advertise them specifically, that
it would in the end of their days fare ill with the wicked,
well with the righteous? This they were assured of before
they left Egypt; only now their knowledge rested on a
broader basis, rose to more majestic proportions, and thrilled
with more terrible foreboding or more gladdened hope. They
had promise of the life that now is, in case of obedience; and
it must have been understood on all hands, that this was but
a pledge and guarantee of acceptance in the life to come with
" the God of the spirits of all flesh" (Numbers xvi. 12;
xxvii. 16). The Lord their God led them the forty years in
the wilderness, that they might know that His Word, and
not bread alone, was their life (Deuteronomy viii. 2, 3). The
man that did God's judgments would " live in them "
(Leviticus xviii. 5). Not merely as not dying a premature
death, or as not continuing to enjoy the material and church
privileges of an Israelite. He would thereby become inheritor
of true, indefectible, and everlasting being with Him whose
Self-originated life is the same yesterday, and to-day, and
for ever. And whatever ecclesiastical disability, or providential visitation of evil, may be carried by that often recurring
and dreadful formula of malediction, " That soul shall be
cut off from his people," or, " cut off from the congregation
of Israel," it cannot but have been intended by Moses to
convey, and it must inevitably have brought home to the

minds of the Israelites, most solemn intimations—none the
less intelligible and moving because not articulated—of a
residuary, final, and far more grievous ban and excision in
the world to come. Indeed, it is not too much to say, that if
the Institute of Moses had nothing to do with a Future Life,
if it did not presuppose, uphold, enlarge, and give new
practical significance to this great article of religion and
morals ; if its sanctions lay wholly within the boundary lines
of the sensible and present; it becomes a colossal and
unwieldy engine for accomplishing a trifle ; it involves an
enormous and unparalleled waste of Divine interference ; and
it is wholly out of keeping, as well with the principles of
God's government of the world, as with the drift and scope
of the Volume which chronicles its history. And thus we
conclude, that implicitly, if not ostensibly, Moses taught
the doctrine of a Future Life with a reality and a force
altogether unexampled in any previous age. At the same
time, let it be noted, that whereas the Scripture Books,
whose testimony we are just now considering, introduce us to
an enlarged world of spiritual beings and agencies—theo-
phanies, good and evil angels, magicians, wizards, and the
like—they distinctly echo the voices which we heard pro-
claiming our doctrine in Genesis, and they add to the witness
new voices of their own. There is the same clear line drawn
between the material and immaterial elements of human
nature. The soul of man is everywhere brought into alliance
with the invisible and the Divine. God, by His Spirit,
dwells in His elect ones. Every Israelite is to be holy,
because Jehovah is holy. Aaron was " gathered," when he
died upon Mount Hor ; and on two occasions God advertised
Moses that, after he had seen the good land from Abarim, he
should be " gathered " unto his people. Twice Sheol casts
its dark shadow upon the record, first as the subterranean

abyss into which Korah and his company went down alive
(Numbers xvi. 30—33); then, figuratively, as the depth at
the foundation of the mountains, whereunto God's anger
burns against transgressors (Deuteronomy xxxii. 22).
And, beside all this, there is another remarkable passage,
which teaches most strongly, that the breath of men's nostrils
is not the total or even the principal part of their existence.
In Deuteronomy xxx. 15—19, Moses, preaching his last
great sermon to Israel, says, "See I have set before thee this
day life and good, and death and evil; in that I command
thee to love the Lord thy God, to walk in his ways, and to
keep his commandments and his judgments.   I call heaven
and earth to record this day against you, that I have set
before you life and death, blessing and cursing: therefore
choose life, that both thou and thy seed may live : that thou
mayest love the Lord thy God : . . . for he is the life and the
length of thy days."

Later on in our inquiry we must call special attention to
this language.   In the earlier Old Testament Books it occurs
only here and in one or two other texts already named.   But
we cannot mistake the speaker's meaning.   Our side lights
must all be put out before we can interpret his words otherwise than as denoting an undefined, but yet most glorious,
lofty, and enduring participation in the being of God to be
enjoyed by all His faithful servants.   And when, in that
awful interview between God and Moses, recorded in Exodus
xxxii. 31 *ff*, Moses prays, that if Israel were not pardoned,
his name, like that of other sinners, might be blotted from
the book which God had written, we have a revelation of
a Future Life of Rewards and Punishments, which, while
it is purely incidental, is as clear as it is blessed and
tremendous.

III. The next stage of our progress carries us through the weary centuries extending from the death of Joshua to the brilliant epoch of David and Solomon—the centuries whose history is written, now in annalistic fragments, and now in connected and vigorous narrative, in the Books of Judges, Ruth, Samuel, and parts of Kings and Chronicles. A Future Life and its realities could hardly be expected to come into prominence amidst the wars, the political distractions, and the shocking irreligion and idolatry, the record of which forms the staple of the documents now mentioned; and the fact is in harmony with the circumstances. This portion of the Old Testament has little to say on our subject. Still, there is the same awful presence of the invisible world, with its superhuman agents and machinery. The Lord of hosts —holy and terrible— dwells between the cherubims (2 Samuel vi., vii.; 1 Chronicles xxi.). His Spirit comes upon men— Othniel, Gideon, Jephthah, Samson, Saul—endowing them with preternatural faculties. A great company of angels, mighty, wise, and benevolent (1 Samuel xxix.; 2 Samuel xiv.; 1 Chronicles xii.), obeys the voice of God. Either by immediate inspiration, or through ministering spirits, God communicates His will to Samuel and others (Judges vi., xiii.; 1 Samuel iii.). Unseen potentates of evil, Divinely allowed, sway the human soul. Satan—here for the first time bearing this odious name—appears as a worker of mischief in the church of God (1 Chronicles xxi.). And miserable creatures, men and women, practise dark arts of witchcraft and magic, and seek to throw a diabolic spell upon the life and wellbeing of their fellows. Now we must contend, that where beliefs like these obtained, and truths like these were known, the doctrine of a separate state of the soul of man, and of moral retribution beyond the grave, cannot have been far distant. And when we remark how this entire cycle of theological and ethical sentiment is only the reproduction and further expansion of what we find in the Pentateuch and Joshua—how the very terminology of the earlier documents presents itself again and again in these later ones—we should outrage the first demands of our reason, if we did not lay it down as certain, that the contemporaries of Deborah, Boaz, and Samuel, however wicked or superstitious, were well acquainted with the dogma of the Future Life, as contained in the books of Moses. If we needed at once illustration and confirmation of this, we have both in the recurrence with variations of the formulas touching the dead, which we found in the older records.   Joshua, and also all that generation, were " gathered unto their fathers " (Judges ii. 8—10).   In like manner, David was told beforehand that he should go the way of all the earth (1 Kings ii. 2), and be with his fathers (1 Chronicles xvii. 11) ; and both he and Solomon, in due time, first slept with their fathers, and then were buried (1 Kings ii. 10 ; 2 Chronicles ix. 31)—language which, to say the least, can have no slighter value than we found it to possess in more ancient Old Testament writings.   Here and there, too, along the line of the narrative, we meet with incidental expressions, which, if they do not prove the doctrines of Futurity and of Retribution, as matters of belief on the part either of the writers or the subjects of the history, are yet, taken in conjunction with all that goes before, very strikingly suggestive of them—so suggestive, that it would be a precarious criticism, which should refuse to recognise their presence.   Standing where the words do—with the lights of Paradise and the shadows of Sinai both upon them—what a significance may we not discover in David's solemn collocation of the life of Jonathan's soul with that of Jehovah ! (1 Samuel xx. 3).   And who does not feel as if the doors of eternity were thrown suddenly open upon him,

as he hears the sweet but solemn music of Hannah's song—
" God shall keep the feet of His saints, and the wicked shall
be silent in darkness " (1 Samuel ii. 9); or the words of
the dying David warning his gifted son and successor—" If
thou seek [the God of thy father], He will be found of thee,
but if thou forsake Him, He will cast thee off for ever"?
(1,Chronicles xxviii. 9.)

But however we may judge in this respect, there is a
passage, hitherto unnoticed, in one of the books now
under review, the witness of which to the doctrine of a
Future Existence, but as held among the Israelites in the
days of their first monarch, and as countersigned by the
authority of Old Testament Scripture, is plain and indubitable. The account which 1 Samuel xxviii. gives of the interview between Saul and the Witch of Endor is conclusive
alike for the one point and the other. Be the philosophy of
witchcraft what it may, clearly Saul and his attendants
believed that men exist after death, and that, in certain
circumstances, they are within call of the living. And
whatever moral or religious difficulties may cumber our
narrative, it is unequivocally pledged to the statement, that
the dead Samuel, in a visible form, and with an audible
voice, carried on a conversation with Saul, rebuking him for
his sins, and predicting his death on the following day—
pledged, therefore, to the affirmation, that a Future Life is a
reality and a fact. Indeed, we catch glimpses here of the
nature of the life after death, as exhibited in the Old
Testament. It would not be safe to argue, that because
Samuel was seen to come up out of the earth, the writer
must therefore have conceived of disembodied souls as
dwelling underground. No doubt this was the popular idea
respecting Sheol *—the hollow place, as the word means—

* The historic connection between the burial of the body in the earth.

and the woman's plans and the expectations of all present framed themselves in accordance with it. But the record does not bind itself to the opinion. It was just what might be looked for, that the miracle should take its form from the circumstances which evoked it; and in representing the buried prophet as rising from the earth, the historian no more endorses the doctrine that the dead are beneath our feet, than Moses affirms in his cosmogony, that there is a solid crystal sphere dividing the waters above and the waters below the firmament. But the narrative does embody dogma. Not only are the dead alive. They are conscious. In particular cases, at least, they have knowledge of human affairs. All men, be their character what it may before God, pass at death into a realm of being, which, however many diversities it may include, possesses certain great features in common. "To-morrow thou," the guilty king, "shalt be with me," the faithful prophet. Last of all, the good, in the state of the soul which immediately follows death, enjoy a tranquillity in comparison with which this mortal life is unrest and disturbance. So much—to say the least—the affecting story of the midnight scene at Endor teaches.

IV, But here, before proceeding further down the course of our inquiries, an Old Testament Book demands attention, which,

and the disappearance of the man would favour the belief. And the language, not only of poetry, but also of ordinary life, might easily frame itself upon this natural concurrence of events. Hence, in passages already referred to, Jacob's grey hairs are spoken of as coming down with sorrow to Sheol; the rebels in the wilderness, supernaturally buried by the visitation of God, go down alive into Sheol; and the sublime song of Moses at the end of Deuteronomy puts Sheol in juxtaposition with the foundations of the mountains. In like manner Hannah (1 Samuel ii. 6) speaks of Jehovah bringing men down to Sheol; and David uses similar terms in his advice to Solomon respecting Shimei (1 Kings ii. 6—9).

while it bears important witness to the doctrine of a Future
Life, has very marked features of its own, and in more than
one respect stands by itself in the Sacred Volume. The Book
is anonymous. The author of it, and the age which produced
it, are alike unknown. The Hebrew in which it is written
has an exceptionally strong Syrian and Arabic colouring, yet
is free from all trace of a mongrel or degenerate dialect.
Unlike the bulk of the Old Testament literature, it connects
itself not so much with Israel as with Edom, Israel's alien
brother and rival. Yet it has always formed part of the Old
Testament Canon, holding in the Jewish arrangement of the
books—an arrangement, as is well known, not strictly chronological—the first place of honour after the Psalms of David
and the Proverbs of Solomon. Its subject is the mystery of
Providence in the affliction of the righteous. And by the
grandeur of its topics, the simple picturesqueness of its
characters, and the wonderful combination of the familiar
and mysterious, the human and Divine, in its incidents, its
images, and its ethical and spiritual doctrines, the Book of
Job is confessedly the most precious composition of its class
to which human thought and language ever gave existence.
It is superfluous to say, that the most various, in some
instances the wildest and most extravagant theories have
been advanced in relation to the authorship and age of this
remarkable work, the prevailing tendency of the modern
criticism being to fix the date of it some centuries later than
the Davidic or Solomonic age. A very ancient tradition
attributes the book to Moses : and we are bold to say,
that, whereas there is nothing in the history, sentiment, style,
or diction of the poem to contravene this view of its origin,
there is much in its structure, its air, and even in its
language, to favour and commend it. Whoever the author
was, he must, at some period of his life, have enjoyed

prolonged opportunity of quiet thought and reflection; he
must have been a man of high culture, and of consummate
ability as a writer; and he must have possessed an unrivalled
command of the resources of the Hebrew tongue. And how
well all this consorts with what we know of the personal
history and literary accomplishments of Moses—his Egyptian
education, his many years' solitary life as a shepherd in the
Sinaitic Peninsula, and his acknowledged mastery both as
a historian and a poet, we need not labour to point out. It
would be presumptuous indeed to affirm, that Moses really did
write the Book of Job. But it cannot be proved that he did
not. There are theories of its authorship abundantly less
tenable. It is far more likely that it came from the pen of
Moses than that it was the production of some great Hebrew
Pascal and Sir Walter Scott in one of the time of Hezekiah,
or even of Solomon. For ourselves we believe it to be the
fruit of the Midian life of Moses—possibly put into its final
form by the illustrious lawgiver not long before his death,
and handed over by him to the custody of Joshua, together
with the other autographs then making up the Book of
God.

But, be this as it may, one thing is sure: the work
breathes throughout the air of the patriarchal and sub-patri-
archal age. The civilization which grows out of the massing
and coalescence of mankind, is not unknown to it; on the contrary, it is distinctly, and sometimes vividly present; but it
never forms the foreground, always stands on the horizon of the
writer's circle of thought and experience. And the theology
of the Book, whether it bears us backward, as it does, to the
cradle of our race, or forward, as it also does, to times far
later than any possible date of its own composition, is,
notably and manifestly, in all its main features, that of the
period extending from about the time of Moses to the epoch

of Samuel, as this theology appears in the last four volumes of the Pentateuch, and in the documents known among the Jews as the Early Prophets.

Hence the doctrine of the Future Life, as it offers itself in the Book of Job, is substantially the same as that which we have traced along the stream of the literature from Exodus to 1 Kings ; only certain aspects of the doctrine come more frequently and luminously into view; and in some cases we have fresh and even startling revelations of what the Shemites of the second ante-Christian millennium believed and knew respecting death and its sequences. The Book everywhere coordinates mankind with that vast assemblage of spiritual beings and agencies, which confronts us at every turn in the earlier Scriptures, and which they and our document agree to exhibit as absolutely independent of the flux and mutations of this world. Unlike the angel-saints, men dwell in houses of clay (iv. 17), and " the cords of their tent " are liable to be cut (iv. 21) ; but the occupants do not perish with their habitation ; their spiritual essence still remains, and is gathered back into the hands of Him whose breath gave it understanding (xxxii. 8 ; xxxiv. 14, 15). Perhaps no one Old Testament book contains more numerous, elaborate, and mournful pictures of the utter and final severance, which death effects between man and all earthly interests ; but it never once suggests, that death is the extinction of our being ; so far from this, it assumes throughout, and often teaches in plain terms, that· men survive themselves, and, though in altered circumstances, live as truly out of the flesh as in the flesh. When men die, their bodies are laid in the grave ; they themselves go to that hidden sphere of the departed, of which Jacob, Moses, Hannah, and David speak under the name of Sheol, and which the Book of Job describes in language precisely similar to theirs, with the poetic variation, perhaps, in a single instance, of adamantine bars in place of the baleful network which compassed David's feet (2 Samuel xxii. 16). Sheol—it is a depth so deep, that God's perfection alone is deeper (Job xi. 8); a mystery so secret, that the hand of God alone can lift the veil which covers it (xxvi. 6). It carries sinners prematurely off, just as the summer's heat makes the snow-water its prey (xxiv. 19). Men without exception go down (vii. 9) and sink into it (xxi. 23); and there, in "the meeting-place of all living"—to use the very language, of the patriarch—they find an abode (xvii. 14), sundered from earth and its concerns by barriers which none can violate (vii. 10, 11; x. 21; xvii. 16). Not that the life of the dead is a neutral, homogeneous state of existence, without distinction of character or circumstances. Whatever else the Book of Job does not teach, it is clear on the subject of future retribution. All men lie down together in the dust; they lie down in Sheol; and so far as this world's doings affect them, they sleep an eternal sleep; but their slumber is a conscious one, and they are not all in the same Providential condition. It is well with the good—how well is not explained; with the evil it is not well. When Zophar says that the wicked perish like the vilest and most odious refuse (xx. 7), it is implied that the good do not so perish: and with the doctrine of Sheol in view, as taught by our document, we must understand him to mean, that the Life to Come is retributive, alike for well-doers and for evil-doers. The punitive character, for the wicked, of the state after death is still more expressly taught, where the sin of men's youth is represented as lying down with them in the dust (xx. 11)—terms which suffer palpable injustice, if they are not explained as conveying, that men suffer hereafter for the sin they have done on the earth. The terrific pictures of the final visitation of God upon those who live only for themselves and for this world, contained in the 18th, 20th, and 27th chapters of our Book, are not simply the creations of Eastern poetry, taking its loftiest and most awful flights. They are more than this. They embody religious sentiment, belief, and fact. When the sinner, overtaken by death, is described as thrust out of a world of light into abysmal darkness (xviii. 18); as smitten through with the wrathful shafts of God's bow of steel (xx. 24); and as opening his eyes in frantic terror to discover that he was and is not (xxvii. 19); and when these representations are found to be emphatically limited to the case of the wicked, it is manifest, that the speakers in the dialogue anticipated a terrible recompense of reward in the life to come for all who did iniquity, and that they were equally clear, that a very different destiny was in reserve for such as wrought righteousness. The hypocrite's hope, when God takes away his soul (xxvii. 8)—where is it? But the hope of the godly—that shall be fulfilled. This is the uniform style and spirit of the Book in relation to the issues of men's life on earth. It presents us with no distinct images either of the felicity or the misery of the world to come; but it intimates most plainly, that human souls after death receive blessing or cursing from God according to their deeds.

The most striking phenomenon of the Book of Job, however, belonging to our topic, remains to be noticed. The Egyptian theology, it is well known, comprehended the dogma of the resurrection of the dead. To this day an extended series of mural paintings, representing the death, burial, and rising again of the great god Osiris, may be seen in an upper chamber of the Isis temple at Philæ; and the practice of embalming was very possibly connected with this article of the Egyptian creed. And here, in the most ancient religious poem in existence, the same doctrine

comes into view, as part of the immeasurably precious stock
of theological ideas possessed in common by the ancient
Hebrews, Aramæans, and Arabs.   The 14th chapter contains
a passage apparently framed upon this sublime sentiment.
The meaning is a little doubtful, and we therefore do not
press it.   But it seems to make Job say, that if God would
only hide him in Sheol till the tempest of His wrath was
overpast, he would patiently wait there till the signal should
be given for his return to earth; so he would hasten back
into the light of God's countenance in the land of the living—
language which, supposing this to be its value, presumes,
on the part of the writer and of the interlocutors in the
poem, at least the possibility, as a conception, that the dead
may come to life again.   But whether the place in question
will sustain this conclusion or no, it clearly intimates the
conscious existence of the soul in a separate state.   And
there is another and more familiar passage of the book, the
evidence of which, in witness to the resurrection of the
dead, we will not say as a Scripture doctrine, but as a
belief of the age in which the author lived, ought not, we
think, to be disputed.   "I know," says Job, "that my
Redeemer liveth, and by-and-by he shall arise upon the
earth; and when, after my skin, this [body] is reduced to
naught, my flesh all gone, I shall behold God: whom I
shall behold myself, and mine own eyes shall see, and not a
stranger, although my reins be utterly consumed within me"
(xix. 25—27).   That no one can be absolutely sure of the
meaning of every portion of this passage, we freely grant;
and it is certain, that more has sometimes been extracted
from it than a rigid criticism could endorse.   But the language, to say the least, is most strongly suggestive of the
hope of resurrection; and we are satisfied, that this is what
it really expresses.   It is not merely that the patriarch is

confident of life beyond the grave. He anticipates the coming of a day—how near or how remote he does not indicate—when, though his mortal frame has wholly vanished in decay, God his Redeemer shall be manifest on earth, and with his very eyes beholding Him, in sight of all his enemies, he shall obtain a solemn vindication of his righteousness. We would not dogmatize. Just now it is our business to decide upon the natural and fairly argued meaning of the words, as belonging to an authentic literary document of ancient times. But we confess, that to explain them simply as if Job wished to say that, long after mortality had done its work with him, God would make his integrity appear, and that, in the realm of spirits, he should be a joyful spectator of the Divine apocalypse on his behalf, is to do meagre justice to the terms in which the patriarch speaks. Earth, not the world of spirits, is the sphere in which Job looks for the future revelation of God: the revelation is to be a physical one, such as the sense could take cognisance of: and, with those around him to witness, who now did him cruel wrong, he knew that he should stand, himself incarnate, before the incarnate champion of his rights, and find acceptance with Him. We repeat it—with no desire to dogmatize or exaggerate, regarding the passage purely in a literary point of view, we judge, that the demands of scientific exposition are only adequately met, when it is taken as implying the speaker's faith in the doctrine of a future resurrection. At least, it will not be denied, that the cast of the passage strongly favours such an interpretation, and that, in any case, it is a most significant and emphatic record of a contemporary belief in the immortality of man.

V. The splendid era of David and Solomon introduces us to a section of the Old Testament literature in which, if anywhere, we might expect to meet with the doctrine of the Future Life. The Davidic and other earlier Psalms,* occupied as they are with the glories of the nature, character, and government of God; and the Solomonic Proverbs and Koheleth, or Ecclesiastes, dealing, the one with maxims of life and the ripe fruits of human experience, the other with philosophic speculations on man's existence and destiny, could scarcely fail to supply important illustrations of our topic. And, as matter of fact, they throw an affluent light upon it. In two of the Books now named, the Psalter and Ecclesiastes, a considerable number of passages may be found—sometimes very incisive and startling ones—of the class referred to in the beginning of this Lecture, passages which seem to affirm, that man at death passes, if not into non-existence, at least into such unconsciousness, that thenceforward he has neither passion, thought, nor sensibility. Thus in the Psalms, those that go down into the pit, and become inhabitants of Sheol, "are no more" (xxxix.). They cannot, as they once did, offer to God thanksgiving (vi.). How shall the dead arise and praise Him? (lxxxviii.) In death there is no remembrance of God, neither any access to Him for them that lie down in silence (xxviii. 6; cxv.). And who has not shuddered as the bitter "Preacher" has led him to the skirts of time, and there, thrusting forth his taper light into the gloom beyond, has whispered in his ear with ghostly voice—"To all there happeneth but one event (Ecclesiastes ii. 14; ix.). The wise man dieth even as the fool (ii. 16). The days of light are few: then follows the long darkness (xi. 8). The dead know nothing: their love,

---

* In what follows Psalms are occasionally quoted, the date of which is probably later than the time of David or Solomon. The later Psalms, however, are so manifestly echoes of the tone, and even of the diction of the older, that, where doctrine is concerned, the anachronism is of little consequence.

hate, all is perished; for in the grave, to which men go, is neither work, device, knowledge, nor wisdom" (ix. 5—10). But where these and similar expressions are not, avowedly or obviously, the outcry of temporary spiritual struggle and bewilderment; or the moan of depression of mind, caused by pain and sorrow; or, again, the reclaim of the natural love of life as against an unknown and untried futurity; the Books themselves are in evidence, that they must be understood with limitation, and that they are not to be made the playthings of a wilful and childish exegesis. The strongest passage of the whole puts the key into our hands, explaining both itself and all the rest. Are dead men nothing? Yes, nothing; for to them—this is the sense in which they are nothing—there is not " any more a portion in anything that is done under the sun" (Ecclesiastes ix. 6). And if we will be still contentious, the ground is wholly cut away from under us—unless, indeed, it may be held, that men like David and Solomon could, within a few lines, write the most patent contradictions—by the distinct and positive teaching on the subject of a Life to Come, which interpenetrates and glorifies each and all of the documents now before us. Whatever minute differences of conception or phraseology may be traceable among them, they all agree substantially in the following doctrines :—

(*a.*) The spirit of man does not die with the body : it returns to God who gave it (Ecclesiastes xii. 7). This doctrine, stated in so many words in Ecclesiastes, underlies the Psalms and Proverbs everywhere, and again and again comes to the surface in forms which cannot be mistaken.

(*b.*) Not simply existence in a future world, but existence in the strict and proper sense of the term—real, desirable, blessed existence—is bound up with Righteousness, or, what is the same thing, with Wisdom, or the Fear of God. Even

Ecclesiastes suggests this sublime dogma (Ecclesiastes viii. 10, 13). It is by no means an unfamiliar presence in the Psalter. As for the Book of Proverbs, it blazes with the light of it. Wicked men have their portion in this life. Time exhausts for them the possibilities of being. They are blotted out of the book of the living (Psalm lxix.; comp. Exodus xxxii. 32). Not so the good (Psalm xvii.). They are gods : they shall not perish like others (Psalm lxxxii.). The way of the ungodly shall perish (Psalm i.) ; the way of the just is the way everlasting (Psalm cxxxix.). Such is the tone of the sacred singers. And if we hesitate to quote the 119th Psalm, intensely Davidic as it is, as being pro-bably one of low date, it is not because its doctrine of the eternity of spiritual understanding was a stranger to the period. Let Solomon testify. The fear of the Lord tendeth to life (Proverbs xix. 23); nay, is a fountain of life (xvi. 27). The supernatural wisdom is Paradise regained ; it is a tree of life, it is life itself to them that receive it (iii. 8 ; iv. 22 ; xi. 30). " Whoso findeth me (Wisdom) findeth life, and shall obtain favour of the Lord " (viii. 35, 36). " The path of the just is as the shining light, that shineth more and more unto the perfect day ;" for " in the way of righteousness is life, and in the pathway thereof is no death" (iv. 18 ; xii. 28).* We will not formally argue, that this language cannot with any reason be taken either literally of length of days, or, by a metaphor, of transcendent temporal good. In either case, notorious facts must have belied the writers' statements to their face, while the very terms which they

* This series of passages is only the reappearance under other forms, sometimes in the very same form, of that dual mystery of life and death, which inaugurates the historic revelation of the Bible, which startles the reader of Leviticus and Deuteronomy in passages quoted a while since, and which we shall again encounter in Ezekiel and others of the Prophets.

employ forbid so poor an application. If eternity be not
eternal, as we sometimes hear, at least it outruns time ; and
whatever else the life ascribed by our documents to righteousness may carry with it, it certainly implies participation, for
the possessors of it, beyond the present world, in the limit-
less existence and supreme felicity of God. The godly have
hope in their end, and their expectation is not cut off
(Proverbs xvi. 32 ; xxiii. 18).

(*c.*) For all men the Future is one of retribution. " God
shall render to every man according to his work " (Psalm
lxii. 12). No doctrine of our Books is more strongly marked
than this. The solemn antitheses of salvation and destruction occur perpetually under aspects, which oblige us to seek
their full and ultimate significance in God's dealings with
men as His servants or His enemies in the world to come.
" When the wicked spring as the grass, and when all the
workers of iniquity do flourish, it is that they shall be
destroyed for ever " (Psalm xcii. 7). " With long life " will
God " satisfy His servants, and will show them His salvation " (Psalm xci. 16). Forgetters of God are liable to be
torn in pieces of Him, but to such as order their conversation aright He will show His salvation (Psalm xlix.). God
is the salvation of His people (Psalm xxv.), but destruction
shall be to the workers of iniquity (Proverbs ix. 29 ; xi. 8) :
they shall be destroyed for ever (Psalm xcii. ; Ecclesiastes
v. 6). To restrict these and other similar expressions,
scattered thickly through the documents, to good lying
wholly within the limits of earth, is an arbitrary fettering of
the sense, such as no reasonable criticism will endure. So
again, while on the one hand it is affirmed and reaffirmed
by our Books, that there is an eventual reward for the
righteous (Psalm xcvii. ; Proverbs xi. 18), the resources of
language are strained to set forth the certainty of the final

visitation of God upon evildoers, and to picture the ruin
past remedy, which overtakes them in their mortal dissolution. The wicked lie under sentence of judgment (Ecclesiastes viii. 11). They are reserved for the day of evil and
destruction (Proverbs xvi. 4; Psalm xcii.). Sooner or later
they die without knowledge (Proverbs v. 22, 23), and are
broken without remedy (Proverbs vi. 15). Their lamp is
put out (Proverbs xiii. 9). They are cut down like grass
(Psalm xxxvii.). Though hand join in hand, they do not go
unpunished (Proverbs xi. 31; xvi. 5). God overthrows
them (Proverbs xxi. 12). He whets His sword and kills
them (Psalm vii.). His angel chases them (Psalm xxxv. 5).
Snares, fire, and brimstone, and burning tempest sweep
them away (Psalm xi.). They are turned into Sheol (Psalm
vii.). They wring out the dregs of the cup of God's indigna-
tion (Psalm lxxv.). The day of their calamity comes at last,
and they perish for ever (Psalm xcii.), amidst the mocking
laughter of the Wisdom which they hated (Proverbs i. 24).
With the righteous it is far otherwise. Righteousness
delivereth from death (Proverbs x. 2; xi. 4). The just have
a sure recompense of blessing (Proverbs xi. 18). Good is
repaid to them (Proverbs xiii. 21). They stand eternally
(Proverbs x. 25). God is their portion for ever (Psalm
lxxiii.). The wicked is driven away in his wickedness, but
the righteous hath hope in his death (Proverbs xiv. 32).
And, what is most worthy of attention, two at least of the
Books speak distinctly of a great assize, at which God will
by-and-by judge mankind in righteousness. We have it in
the Psalms. "The Lord . . . . hath prepared His throne for
judgment; and He shall judge the world in righteousness"
(Psalm ix. 8, 9; xcvi.; xcviii.). "The wicked shall not
stand in the judgment, nor sinners in the congregation of
the righteous: for the Lord knoweth the way of the righteous,

but the way of the ungodly shall perish " (Psalm i.).   So
again, with wonderful explicitness, in Ecclesiastes.   God
requires the past (iii. 15), and will judge the righteous and the
wicked (iii. 17).   He will bring men into judgment for their
ways ; yea, every work will He judge, with every secret
thing, whether it be good or evil (xi. 9 ; xii. 4).   Indeed,
there are passages in the Psalms and Proverbs, which out-
strip this threefold doctrine, and anticipate the sublimest
and most distinctive teaching of the New Testament on the
subject of the last things.   In the 17th Psalm, David con-
gratulates himself, that his destiny was not that of men of
the world ; he should behold the face of God in righteousness, and, when he woke up, should be satisfied with the
revelation of Jehovah's image.   "Guide me with Thy
counsel," is the prayer of Asaph, " and afterwards take me,"
—even as Thou tookest Enoch, is his meaning—" to glory "
(Psalm lxxiii.).   In like manner a Korahite Psalm declares,
that God will redeem His servants from the grave, for He
will take them (Psalm xlix.).   On the contrary, a second
voice of the Korahite tells us, that wicked men go to the
darkness, where death is the shepherd of the sheep, and
where no light of morning ever dawns (*ib.*).   And, in awful
unison, we hear the oracle of Solomon : " The man that
wandereth out of the way of understanding shall remain in
the congregation of the dead " (Proverbs xxi. 16).   Language this, which, after making all deduction for the doubtful value of words, or the boldness of Eastern metaphor,
incontestably contains the doctrine of eternal blessedness with
God, if not also that of its tremendous opposite, while, at the
same time, to say the least, it adumbrates, in a very remarkable manner, the Christian dogma of the resurrection of the
just.   Indeed, it is not going too far to affirm that the three
Books of Psalms, Proverbs, and Ecclesiastes must be

deliberately and persistently read backwards, if a future state of retributive reward and punishment for man is not found in them.

VI. The latter half of the 1st Book of Kings, the 2nd Book of Kings, and the 2nd of Chronicles, taken up as they are with the annals of the double line of monarchs who, for three or four centuries after the death of Solomon, ruled his divided empire, make but small contribution to the material of our present inquiry. They furnish copious illustration of the idolatry, superstition, and licentiousness which, alike in church and state, became the normal character of both sections of Israel. They perpetually bring into view the doctrines of the moral perfection of God; of sin as a high crime and misdemeanour against the Divine Majesty; and of the reality of a Providence which, sooner or later, deals with all men according to their works. They also contain instructive teaching as to the influence and operation of Jehovah's Spirit, as to the character and offices of angels, and as to other points of Old Testament theology. But beyond the monotonous record, that this or that king "slept with his fathers," or, as we find it less frequently, "slept with his fathers and was buried," or, in a single instance, "was gathered to his fathers," the sacred scribes of the monarchies seldom carry us beyond the frontiers of this world; and they add nothing to the voices of the unseen and future, which speak through the lute of David, or the philosophic tongue of Solomon.

With the contemporary series of Prophets, however, it is otherwise. Here we not only meet, under pronounced and impressive forms, with the now familiar doctrines of the spiritual nature of God, of the immateriality of the soul, of the marvellous agency of Him whom Isaiah calls God's Holy Spirit, of the equivalence of righteousness and life in man, of moral retribution, and of Sheol; but, particularly in the older pre-Exilian prophets—Isaiah, Joel, Hosea, Amos, Jonah, and others—the Future World and its conditions, stand forth with a clearness and grandeur, such as more than once transcend all previous representations of Scripture concerning them. We do not say, that the passages alluded to must be taken, in every instance, as binding their authors to a categorical affirmation of the doctrines embodied in them. But if this could not be maintained, they at least argue a general knowledge and belief of such dogmas in the times and countries to which the prophets belonged. Thus the magnificent lyric which Isaiah, in the 14th chapter of his Prophecy, puts by anticipation into the mouth of liberated Israel—a lyric unrivalled in literature for sublime personification and annihilating satire—while, by its very nature, it spurns the strict lines of logic and theology, yet in making Sheol move at the coming of the Babylonian monarch, and stir her dead kings from their thrones to go forth and taunt him, bears sure witness, that the Prophet's language was in keeping with the prevalent faith of his people, and that both he and they were familiar with the conception, not only of the invisible being, but also of the intelligence and possible activity, of departed human souls.

Still more striking are the passages in which both Isaiah and Hosea speak of the abolition of death, and of the resurrection of the dead. "In this mountain"—that is, of Jerusalem—says Isaiah (xxv. 6—8), "the Lord of hosts . . . . . will swallow up death in victory, and . . . . will wipe away tears from off all faces." So of the Israel of Samaria Hosea writes (xiii. 14) : "I will ransom them from the grave; I will redeem them from death : O death, I will be thy plagues; O grave (Sheol), I will be thy destruction : repentance shall be hid from Mine eyes." To the same effect

Isaiah in another place (xxvi. 19—21) apostrophizes Judah
in these remarkable terms: "Thy dead men shall live,
together with my dead body shall they arise. Awake and
sing, ye that dwell in dust: for thy dew is as the dew of
herbs, and the earth shall cast out the dead. . . . . The Lord
cometh out of His place to punish the inhabitants of the earth
for their iniquity : the earth also shall disclose her blood, and
shall no more cover her slain." Now here we must repeat
that, confining ourselves within the limits prescribed by the
sternest exegesis, our passages are distinctly in proof that,
in the eighth century before Christ, the people of Palestine,
among whom Isaiah and Hosea lived, were acquainted with
the dogma of the Resurrection of the Dead. But this is not
all. These latter passages put us in advance of the prophetic
ode on the downfall of the King of Babylon. They are the
language of distinct anticipation and promise. Isaiah and
Hosea are committed to the doctrine. At least, we do not
see how it can be otherwise. No doubt their words are, to a
certain extent, figurative. The Divine disannulling of death,
the refusal of the earth to act any longer as the gaoler of
human dust, and the joyful awaking and song of the
denizens of the grave, may be explained as highly wrought
metaphors, used to describe the felicitous change which
should pass upon Israel when God brought them home
from Babylon. But how of the metaphors themselves?
Whence did they come? If the prophets Isaiah and Hosea
illustrate a future revival of Israel by the image of dead
men springing up alive out of their graves, it is reasonable
to suppose, that the dogma of the resurrection lay at the
basis of their imagery, and that, in point of fact, they affirm
that, by-and-by, the Israel of the sepulchres, as well as
of the daylight, should share in the glory of the latter times.
It is more than probable, that a similar background of doctrine,

and, we may add, a like forecast of fact, in connection with the last things, are to be traced in Joel's " great and terrible day of the Lord," and in that shuddering soliloquy of the Jewish evildoers in Isaiah (xxxiii. 14)—" Who among us shall dwell with the devouring fire? who among us shall dwell with everlasting burnings?" And although the writings of Zephaniah, Habbakuk, Jeremiah, and other later prophets of the pre-Exile period, contain no such passages as those just quoted, they are in full accord with the earlier documents in their suggestions of a retributive good or evil for man, under the moral government of God, which it would be critical hardihood indeed to restrict within the boundaries of human life and of this world.

VII. The earlier of the two great prophets of the Captivity, Ezekiel, transfers us to a spiritual sphere, differing somewhat from that in which his predecessors utter their voices. Mysterious visions of God present themselves to our gaze; and a novel spiritual symbolism, at once gorgeous and awful —living creatures, and orbs, and eyes, and rushing wings— meet us again and again along the course of his writings. The explanation is probably to be sought in the circumstances of the prophet. At every turn he found himself confronted, in the land of his bondage, with strange emblems and images of celestial things, the handiwork of that ancient Chaldæan and Assyrian religion, which, amidst manifold debasements and corruptions, had preserved so many precious elements of primeval revelation—the very emblems and images, possibly, some of them, which we ourselves at this day see with amazement in the statues, bas-reliefs, cylinders, and gems, brought from the Tigris and Euphrates, and stored in our National Museum. These mystic representations of the unseen, cognate as they were in some respects to the sacred symbols of the Mosaic Institute itself, doubtless threw open to Ezekiel and to others of the Jewish captives fresh realms of religious thought and contemplation. And the Spirit of God, it would seem, conforming His operations, as of old, to the mental state of His elect servant, employed these significant signs, in subordination to those of the Jewish temple and oracle, as instruments of new revelation to the prophet touching God and His providence—the earthly elements of the apocalypse being sorted, cleansed, sublimed, and glorified into that Divine consistency, unity, and majesty, which we mark with dazzled admiration in the record.

But the apocalypse itself, whatever account we may give of its origin and form, presumes and discloses a spiritual world, with whose constitution, agencies, and illimitable being man is essentially connected. It is, in fact, a revelation of the immateriality and immortal destiny of man. What were the wheels of beryl, and the flaming amber light, and the terrible crystal of the cherub-lifted firmament, and the likeness of a throne as the appearance of a sapphire-stone, to Ezekiel and his contemporaries—what are they to us—if human existence is no more than we see it to be? The mystical visions of Chebar declare, and were intended to declare, that human history, character, and life are all linked to the unseen and everlasting, and that here alone they find both their true interpretation and their absolute issues.

But Ezekiel's doctrine of a Hereafter is not chiefly that which the visions suggest. Nor does it lie in the occurrence in his Prophecy—in the famous passage, namely, respecting the valley of dry bones (xxxvii. 1—14)—of language and imagery which, like the texts already cited from Isaiah and Hosea, suppose and are built upon belief in a future resurrection of the dead—though this is a deeply interesting fact, and one not to be overlooked in our argument. But what is most noteworthy is the employment by the prophet, from the beginning of his Book to the end of it, of terms in relation to human character, condition, and destiny, which are only explicable on the principle, that men exist after death, and that their existence is coupled with consummate good or evil according to the manner in which they have lived in the flesh. The terms referred to are " life " and " death." They are not, as we have seen, peculiar to Ezekiel. Setting aside the historical paragraph in which they are found at the beginning of Genesis, they occur for the first time in two or three didactic passages of the Pentateuch already cited (Leviticus xviii. 5; Deuteronomy viii. 2, 3; xxx. 15—19), and they reappear at intervals along the descending line of the Sacred Books. And as we have had occasion to remark, wherever they are found, they point to sanctions and destinies, transcending all merely earthly calamity or blessedness. But in no part of the Old Testament are they employed as in Ezekiel. Here they are pervasive, and the meaning of them is fixed beyond all possibility of doubt. Thus in the third chapter it is said, that a wicked man, whom God warns in vain of the consequences of his evil doing, shall die in his iniquity, while the righteous, maintaining his righteousness, shall live and not die (ver. 17—21). The 18th chapter rings the changes over and over on the same doctrine : " The soul that sinneth, it shall die. But if a man be just, and do that which is lawful and right, he shall surely live . . . saith the Lord God." And again, in the 20th chapter, the statutes and judgments of God are thrice characterised as ordinances " which if a man do, he shall even live in them " (xx. 11, 13, 21). Now, who does not feel, that the exegesis which should interpret this language, either literally of physical life and death, or figuratively of temporal prosperity and adversity, is limping and inadequate? Nay, who does not see that it is false alike to reason and to matter of fact? When was it ever true, unless in very rare and exceptional instances, that men's righteousness or unrighteousness determined the triumph or ruin of their worldly schemes and undertakings— still less the continuance or cessation of their natural life? When could it be true, God's government of the world being what it is? But Ezekiel himself anticipates his expositors. In the thirty-third chapter of his Prophecy we read: " Again the word of the Lord came unto me, saying, Son of man, speak to the children of thy people, and say unto them, When I bring the sword upon a land, if the people of the land take a man of their coasts, and set him for their watchman : if when he seeth the sword come upon the land, he blow the trumpet, and warn the people; then whosoever heareth the sound of the trumpet, and taketh not warning; if the sword come, and take him away, his blood shall be upon his own head. . . . But he that taketh warning shall deliver his soul. But if the watchman see the sword come, and blow not the trumpet, and the people be not warned ; if the sword come, and take any person from among them, he is taken away in his iniquity ; but his blood will I require at the watchman's hand. *So thou, O son of man, I have set thee a watchman unto the house of Israel; therefore thou shalt hear the word at My mouth, and warn them from Me.* When I say unto the wicked, O wicked man, thou shalt surely die; if thou dost not speak to warn the wicked from his way, that wicked man shall die in his iniquity ; but his blood will I require at thine hand. Nevertheless, if thou warn the wicked of his way to turn from it; if he do not turn from his way, he shall die in his iniquity ; but thou hast delivered thy soul. . . . When the righteous turneth from his righteousness, and committeth iniquity, he shall even die thereby. But if the wicked turn from his wickedness, and do that which is lawful and right, he shall live thereby " (ver. 1—19). Now here, it will be observed, the prophet uses the terms " life " and " death," taken in their ordinary, natural sense, by way of illustration. In time of war the watchfulness of the sentinel on the one hand, or his negligence on the other, will often make the difference of the preservation or loss of life to those whom it is his business to guard. And in like manner, God says by Ezekiel, wicked men, who, because they are wicked, are liable to " death," may die or may not die, according as the watcher for souls, appointed to warn and evangelize them, is faithful or faithless to his trust. Thus then there is a life and a death of which the physical conditions so called are but suggestions and symbols—a life and a death which connect themselves essentially and universally with men's moral attitude and behaviour towards God—affecting not their corporeal but their spiritual existence; the undefined and ineffable blossoming and perfection, or else the final blight and uttermost miscarriage, of their very being; all, indeed, that " life " and " death " could mean, the words being translated into the unknown language of the world whose inhabitants are not of flesh. So does Ezekiel teach the doctrine of a separate state of the soul, and of a retributive Hereafter for man; echoing in fact, only with greater distinctness than his prophetic predecessors, the teaching of Moses in the Desert of Sinai and on the Plains of Moab, that teaching itself being but the embodiment, as dogma, of the first communication ever addressed to mankind by the God who made us.

VIII. Our doctrine, as it is seen in Daniel, the second chief prophet of the Captivity, rises to a lofty stature, and assumes a definiteness of form and a brilliancy of colouring altogether without precedent in the Holy Volume. More frequently

and conspicuously, perhaps, than in any other prophet, the
spiritual world, with its direct relations to man, appears
above the horizon in the Book of Daniel.   It is a marked
characteristic of the Book.   So, too, in more than one significant passage the saints of the Most High, as the prophet
calls the godly of mankind, are associated with the eternity
and immortality of God (vii.) in a manner which argues
that, in the prophet's thought, they are as deathless as the
glorious Being whom they serve.   But he towers to an
infinite height above all implication and logical sequence,
and, in language of matchless sublimity, forecasting some of
the noblest revelations of Christianity itself as to the future
of the world and of man, puts a diadem of glory upon the
Old Testament doctrine of the Future Life.   Hear him.   " I
beheld till the thrones were cast down, and the Ancient of
days did sit, whose garment was white as snow, and the
hair of His head like the pure wool : His throne was like the
fiery flame, and His wheels as burning fire.   A fiery stream
issued and came forth from before Him : thousand thousands
ministered unto Him, and ten thousand times ten thousand
stood before Him : the judgment was set, and the books
were opened. . . . I saw in the night visions, and, behold,
One like the Son of man came with the clouds of heaven,
and came to the Ancient of days, and they brought Him near
before Him.   And there was given Him dominion, and
glory, and a kingdom, that all people, nations, and lan-
guages, should serve Him : His dominion is an everlasting
dominion, which shall not pass away, and His kingdom that
which shall not be destroyed " (vii. 9—14).   And again, in
the last chapter of his Prophecy, he says : " And at that
time shall Michael stand up, the great prince which standeth
for the children of thy people : and there shall be a time of
trouble, such as never was since there was a nation even to

that same time: and at that time thy people shall be delivered, every one that shall be found written in the book. And many of them that sleep in the dust of the earth shall awake, some to everlasting life, and some to shame and everlasting contempt. And they that be wise shall shine as the brightness of the firmament; and they that turn many to righteousness as the stars for ever and ever" (xii. 1—3). These passages, so clearly and expressly containing the doctrines of the Resurrection of the Dead and of the General Judgment, have been an intolerable scandal to disbelievers in Divine Revelation; and they have left no means untried to discredit their authenticity, or, at least, to pare down their seemingly preternatural grandeur to merely human dimensions. A common theory supposes, that the prophet borrowed his ideas from the theology of the Persians, and that Zoroaster and the Zendavesta are really the fountain of these surprising rhapsodies. Now we do not care, in reply, to press the objection, that the era of Zoroaster, and the date of the writings with which his name is associated, are quite unsettled; that in fact no one can be sure of the latter, to say nothing of the former, within several centuries. We will grant at once, that in the days of Darius Hystaspis, nay long before the elder Cyrus, all through Mesopotamia and the countries stretching eastward to the frontiers of India, the leading dogmas known as the Zoroastrian—Time without Bounds, Ormazd and Ahriman, the Amshaspands, Judgment to come, the Resurrection of the Dead, Heaven and Hell—were a common possession, derived from an undefined antiquity, and that Daniel in Babylon, therefore, had full opportunity of becoming acquainted with the doctrines now in question as taught in his Prophecy. But what proof is there that Daniel drew upon Parsism for these doctrines, or for any other doctrines contained in his Book? There is no

one of them—take for instance the doctrine of angels—
which may not be found in more than substance and embryo
in earlier Old Testament writings.   And if, as in the case of
Ezekiel, the new religious sphere of the prophet's life gave a
certain complexion to his inspired thoughts and teaching,
this is the most that can be rationally granted to a scientific
criticism.   One thing is indubitable—if the Parsi doctrines
of the Judgment and the Resurrection of the Dead, as they
obtained in the days of Daniel, were not, in point of clearness and dignity, very much in advance of these same
doctrines, as they appear in the Vendidad and other ancient
Zoroastrian books which have come down to our time, it is
wholly unexplained, how they could give the expansion and
elevation, demanded by the hypothesis, to the views on these
subjects, which Daniel must have brought with him to
Babylon from the land of his nativity.   With respect to the
Resurrection, very little is said of it in the Zendavesta.   It
is referred to, and taken for granted, but it is not discoursed
upon or described.   And as to the Judgment, which, according to Parsi opinion, follows close upon death, take the
following passage from the Khordah Avesta : " Praise to the
Omniscience of God, who . . . effects freedom from hell at
the bridge (Chinavad), and leads it over to the brilliant,
fragrant Paradise of the pure. . . . I enter on the shining
way.   May the fearful terror of hell not overcome me!
May I step over the bridge Chinavad!   May I attain to
Paradise, where are much perfume, and all enjoyments, and
all brightness!   Praise to the Overseer, the Lord, who
rewards those who do good deeds according to the will
of Him who purifies at last the obedient, yea delivers the
wicked out of hell."*   Or take the much older paragraph

* Slightly altered from Bleeck's English Translation of Spiegel's
Avesta.   Vol. iii. p. 15.

of the Vendidad—certainly the most striking and typical passage in all the Zendavesta relating to Future Judgment and Retribution :—

"Then answered Ahuramazda (Ormazd) : After the man is dead, after the man is departed, after his going, the wicked, evil-knowing Daevas (Demons) do work,

" In the third night, after the coming and lighting of the dawn.

" And when the victorious Mithra places himself on the mountains with pure splendour,

" And the brilliant sun arises,

" Then the Daeva, Vizaresho by name, O holy Zarathustra (Zoroaster), leads away in bonds the souls of the sinful-living, the wicked, Daeva-worshipping men.

" To the ways created by Time comes he who is godless, and he who is holy :

" To the bridge Chinavad come the created of Ahuramazda, where they interrogate the consciousness and the soul concerning that which was done

" In the corporeal world.

"Thither comes the beautiful, well-created, swift, and well-formed soul,

" Accompanied by a dog.* . . .

"This leads away the souls of the pure over Haraberezaiti (Elborj);

" Over the bridge Chinavad it brings the host of the heavenly Yazatas (Izads—beings worthy of adoration).

---

* According to Parsi notions, a man's dog, if ill-treated in this world, will oppose his passage over the bridge Chinavad in the next. On the other hand, the soul will be helped by the dog, when the creature has received kindness (Wilson on the Parsi Religion, pp. 252, 338). The Gujerati Translation of our text, however, makes the dog to be the children, labour, and good actions of a man, which attend him in this animal form (Bleeck's Spiegel, Vol. i. p. 141).

"Ahumano (The Lordly Intelligence) rises from his golden throne.

"Ahumano speaks : How hast thou, O Pure, come hither,

" From the perishable world to the imperishable world?

" The pure souls go contented

" To the golden thrones of Ahuramazda, of the Ameshaspentas (Amshaspands),

" To Garonmanem (Highest Heaven), the dwelling of Ahuramazda, the dwelling of the Ameshaspentas, the dwelling of the other pure (spirits). . . .

" The pure men are together with him." *

How of passages like these set side by side with the magnificent and solemn descriptions of our prophet? Not only must we read between the lines in wondrous fashion, but, on occasion, we must keep our eyes fast shut, if in this motley combination of truth and falsehood, of things mean, things weird, and things grotesque, we will discover the prototype of that which Daniel saw in the visions of God. It is an affront upon our intellect—to say nothing of our sense of reverence—to collocate the two. Here at least, if reason will be rational, it must needs judge, that that Divine Spirit, at whose instance Daniel, in common with the other Israelitish prophets, claimed to speak, used him, after a supernatural manner past all definition in language, as a chosen and Providentially adapted instrument for unveiling to mankind, with new breadth, explicitness, and pomp of revelation, the counsels of God concerning the last times.

And so the lips of the Old Testament utter as nearly as possible their latest, actually their loudest and clearest, voice on the subject of this Lecture. Ezra, Haggai, Zechariah, Nehemiah, Malachi, Daniel's contemporaries or successors,

* Vendidad, Fargard xix.; Bleeck's Spiegel, Vol. i., p. 141. Compare Wilson, p. 338.

agree with him in their doctrine of God, and of the spiritual world, and of the human soul; but, with a rare exception or two, they make no reference to a Hereafter. Nehemiah, indeed (ix. 29), repeats the old and blessed doctrine, that obedience to God's commandments carries life in its train; and Malachi rings the warning bell announcing the great and terrible day of Jehovah. But Daniel fixes the crown alike upon their witness and upon that of all who rank before them up the sacred ascent of Old Testament record. The coming of the Ancient of days on the judgment throne, and the awaking of the dead generations of men to eternal dishonour or glory— this is the supreme affirmation of our documents as to the Life to Come and its realities.

IX. So far, then, we have accomplished our task. Regarding the Old Testament Scriptures simply as a body of ancient writings; assuming only their authenticity and substantial genuineness; not ignoring the claims of their authors to be supernaturally inspired, still less taking the egregiously unscientific ground of denying the possibility of such inspiration; at the same time setting aside every kind of external authority as a rule of judgment concerning the Volume, and dealing with it, as any other record of antiquity might be dealt with, on the basis of its contents only, fairly and impartially considered; we have endeavoured, by a careful historic and analytic scrutiny, to ascertain how far it recognises the existence of a Future Life, and, where it does this, to determine what representations it makes respecting it. And thus we are prepared to exhibit in few words the entire doctrine of the World to Come, as it appears in the Old Testament, the witness of the Volume being taken in the purely scientific manner just described. No doubt, even among the Egyptians, Chaldeans, Assyrians, Persians, and

other ancient peoples, whose history dovetails with that of
Israel, the doctrine of the Future State—plainly no monopoly
of Israel—was held with an amplitude and a detail greater
than any which our documents expressly attribute to it.*
Apart from the independent evidence of history and extant
monuments—such, for instance, as that which the arrow-
headed inscriptions of Nineveh and the lower Euphrates
are just now so unexpectedly furnishing—the Old Testament
itself supplies hints and glimpses abundantly warranting
this conclusion.   And it would be wholly unjustifiable to tie
down the acquaintance which Israel, either in earlier or later
ages, had with the subject of the Future Life to the absolute
letter of the Sacred Text.   To say nothing of the so-called
Apocryphal Books, of the Targums, the Talmud, and the
ancient Liturgies in use among the Jews—all teeming with
proof that the lines of Hebrew and Aramæan Scripture in
no wise comprehend the total knowledge and belief of Israel
touching a Hereafter—the nature of the case is strongly
against any such idea.   The history of Israel being what we
know it to have been, it is absolutely certain that the doctrine of the Future Life, as the documents deliver it, is but
a sample and imperfect image of a faith extending much
beyond the limits of the record.

But, confining ourselves to the very testimony of our
Volume, and distinguishing, so far as may be, between that
part of the doctrine of the Life to Come for which the Old
Testament writers ought not to be considered responsible,

---

* Profoundly interesting illustration of this statement may be found
in the Chaldean Account of the Deluge, recently discovered among the
Assyrian Cuneiform Tablets of the British Museum, by Mr. George
Smith, and translated by him in the " Transactions of the Society of
Biblical Archæology," Vol. ii. p. 1.   See also Mr. Fox Talbot's Translation, in the same number of the " Transactions," of the Assyrian Legend
of the Goddess Ishtar's Descent into Hades.

and that which they expressly or by plain implication make their own, we find in general that the Hebrew Scriptures assume and teach—(1.) That the human soul continues to live when the body dies. (2.) That the soul at death goes into Sheol, or the invisible world, the descriptions given of this world being generally suggestive of gloom and terror. (3.) That it is well or ill with men after death according to the character of their earthly life. (4.) That obedience to God's commandments is tantamount to immortality. (5.) That God will eventually bring both the quick and the dead into judgment before Him. (6.) That, by the Divine pre-ordination, the terminus of human history will be the absolute catastrophe of evil, the complete triumph and ascendancy of the righteous government of God, and the perfect and everlasting bliss of all holy creatures. This doctrine—dimly discernible, yet most assuredly present, in the earliest Old Testament books; often wholly out of sight through large spaces of the Volume, then coming into view again; now to appearance vague, equivocal, tremulous, flickering, yet in reality never absolutely inconsistent with itself; here gleaming like a thin taper light, and there blazing out with a radiance too glorious to look upon; visibly or invisibly advancing always by a stedfast progress towards a perfection itself imperfect; infinitely loftier and purer, even in its weakness, than the corresponding article of any other ancient religion; manifold and diverse indeed, yet also one and uniform; stamped from first to last, under every disguise, with the signature of a superhuman pedigree—is in brief the doctrine of Old Testament Scripture on the subject of the Future Life, as determined by investigation of the kind above specified.

III.

But the goal is not reached. Hitherto we have spoken with reserve, as under bonds. Now we throw off our bonds. The Old Testament is not an ancient book of religion merely, like the Hindu Shastras, or the Sermons of Gotama Buddha —a book the meaning of which, like that of any other of its class, ends with itself, and is accessible to all men through the ordinary media of intellect, learning, and study. We are not unaware, that it is often regarded as having this purely human character. Nay, it is laid down as a principle by the naturalistic criticism of our day, that it must be so regarded ; that it is fanatical and absurd to regard it otherwise ; and that the expositor, who proceeds on a different basis from this, will land in a transcendental chaos of subjective illusion and reverie. Such is the position—a position, however, which we peremptorily decline to accept. As believers in the supernatural, we decline it. Above all, we decline it as Christians. Were this doctrine true, there never would have been either a New Testament, or a Christ. The Gospel is inexplicable—we may add indefensible also—on this purely scientific hypothesis. How did Christ and His Apostles regard the Old Testament? How did they deal with it? With them it was a supernatural book, having a supernatural significance, comprehensible only through supernatural organs and instruments. Not only was it all true, as any simply human composition might be; its writers spake as they were moved by the Holy Ghost, and its contents were given by inspiration of God. Its facts were parable and allegory. Its personages were emblems, types, and symbols. Its institutions were sermons. Its prophecy wrapped up in it the everlasting thoughts of God. It was a volume of mystery, hidden from the ages and

generations which witnessed the production of it; unsearchable even to the very men who wrote it; known to the
Christian apostles and prophets only by the revelation of the
Divine Spirit; and for ever veiled from all human eyes
which God Himself does not purge to discern its real teaching. Who has not remarked, again and again, how the New
Testament finds Christ in the Old where He is not obvious;
how it gives startling turns to passages, the context of which
seems to cry out as if in pain under the process; how, as in
the case of St. Paul's two famous arguments respecting the
blessing of the world by Abraham's individual seed, and the
universal sovereignty of the Son of Man as taught by the
8th Psalm, it presses a single word to the uttermost; how
it makes points of almost microscopic minutiæ of phraseology;
how it modifies, enlarges, lifts to a new altitude of meaning,
and, after a fashion entirely its own, recasts and beatifies
the ancient record? Scepticism makes quick account of all
this. If it is not deliberate falsification, it is traditional
blundering, and hopelessly unscientific exegesis. The wild
humours of Oriental imagination are seen disporting themselves in the livery of Western dogma and logic. Even
men, who would deem the charge of unbelief an affront and
an injustice, make bold to affirm, that the New Testament
caricatures and travesties the Old. Thus one of the most
advanced of modern English Biblicists, in his recent work
"On a Fresh Revision of the English Old Testament,"
writes (p. 76): "It is acknowledged by scholars, that the
New Testament does not furnish an infallible hermeneutical
standard. The sense it attaches to passages in the Old is
not necessarily correct. The Christian writers usually
followed the Septuagint, or adapted the words of the Jewish
Scriptures to a purpose other than the original one. . . . The
injurious effects," the writer adds, "of such exegesis con-

tinue till the present day." This is plain speaking; and on the naked ground of Science, strictly so called, we do not see our answer. Nor are we careful to see it. Enough, that if Science fails us, Reason does not. There is a broad distinction here, though it is often overlooked. Science is concerned with the physical only. Physical phenomena, physical operations, physical forces—these are the domain of Science. All beyond this—the spiritual, the supernatural, the Divine—Science knows nothing of it. Where miracle begins, Science ends. Not so with Reason. Reason does not exclude Science, much less is it in conflict with it. On the contrary, it recognizes and honours, but at the same time outstrips it. Reason travels with Science to its last frontiers, and there leaves it behind, and soars away far out of its reach. Reason ranges through a universe of realities, in comparison of which the sphere of Science is but a pinpoint.* Times without number the *How* of Science is the *What* of Reason; and Reason would call herself fool to raise the Scientific question. We appeal from Science to Reason. Let it be supposed, not only that the writers of the Old Testament were preternaturally aided by the Holy Spirit, nor even that the Spirit through them conveyed to man preternatural revelations. Let it further be supposed, that these revelations were of set purpose, for moral and spiritual ends, so framed as to be wholly or in part undiscoverable except by the same preternatural influence which at first communicated them—the meaning of some of them being designedly hidden from their writers, nay from all men for

---

* At the recent Meeting of the British Association for the Advancement of Science, held in Belfast, Professor Tyndall, in his Inaugural Address as President, is reported to have said, that where Science and Theology come in conflict, it is no longer an open question, that the latter must give way. In the name of Reason, we protest against the wrong which this dictum does to the ancient and honourable name of Science.

centuries after they were written ; the meaning of the whole
being in perpetuity a blank or a puzzle to human intelligence,
where miracle did not come in aid of nature. Would not
the New Testament be at once intelligible on such a sup-
position? And might not Christ, and the whole system of
Christian verity, follow as a necessary sequence? Now it is
this very principle, on which the New Testament proceeds
in its interpretation of the Old. Its authors claiming—and
surely on irrefragable evidence—to speak by inspiration of
the same Spirit who dictated the ancient Scripture, declare
authoritatively what that Scripture meant, first "opening"
and then "alleging" the things, which we and the whole
Christian world receive as the true sayings of God. Do
we wonder if the exposition surprises us—if our trusted
canons of "historico-grammatical" interpretation are ignored
and trodden under foot; if the Spirit of God in the younger
volume tells us, that His thought in the older was not what
the letter seems to indicate, but something marvellously
deeper and more far-reaching, perhaps totally unlike in kind
and nature? This may not approve itself to Science, but it
will to Reason. Reason sees clearly enough, that Christ,
the Eternal Word made flesh, in whom the Spirit of God
dwelt without measure, is the answer to every objection
raised by the treatment which the Old Testament receives at
the hands of the New—indeed to every scientific objection,
pure and simple, which can be alleged against the earlier
Bible. What is the geological difficulty of the Mosaic Cosmogony, or the chronological difficulty of the many-centuried
lives of the patriarchs, or the philological difficulty of
Deuteronomy or Daniel, in competition with the person and
character of Christ? Christ is pledged to the Divine inspiration of the Old Testament; and this simple fact, for
those who believe in Him, reduces all scientific enigmas to

the imponderable value of the small dust of the balance. "I thank Thee, O Father, Lord of heaven and earth, because Thou hast hid these things from the wise and prudent, and hast revealed them unto babes. Even so, Father: for so it seemed good in Thy sight" (Matthew xi. 25, 26). "Then opened He their understanding, that they might understand the Scriptures" (Luke xxiv. 45). Here is the key to the Old Testament. Like nature and providence, it means much more than it says. It speaks one language to the ear, and another to the soul. From the time of the first writing of it until now, the Spirit of God has reserved to Himself the prerogative of unsealing its mysteries. Itself a miracle, it never was understood, and never will be understood, without another miracle. First the miracle of the Book. Then the miracle of the Eyes. "Open Thou mine eyes, that I may behold wondrous things out of Thy law" (Psalm cxix. 18).

And this principle puts a new face upon the doctrine of the Future Life as well as upon other teachings of the Old Testament. The doctrine may be present, where it is not conspicuous, nay, where, without the supernatural key, we should be quite unable to detect it. What trace is there of its presence in the narrative of the Flood? Yet St. Peter, expounding the narrative, tells us that Christ, by Noah, preached a gospel of everlasting Salvation to the condemned antediluvians. To use his own words—though adjudged to "die according to men in the flesh," opportunity of repentance was given them; they might "live according to God in the Spirit" (1 Peter iii. 17; iv. 6). "I am the God of Abraham, the God of Isaac, and the God of Jacob," was the awful revelation to Moses from the flaming bush (Exodus iii. 6). Does this language teach the resurrection of the dead? Christ shows that it does. "God is not the God of the dead, but of the living" (Luke xx. 37, 38).

Jehovah made promise to Israel in the wilderness, that they should go into His rest (Deuteronomy xii. 9). Into Palestine, that is to say. But not Palestine only, or chiefly. God's rest, as the Epistle to the Hebrews points out, is that everlasting Sabbatism, on which He entered when the works of the days were ended ; and this, not Palestine, was the soul and scope of the promise. It was a promise of Heaven to all faithful Israelites (Hebrews iv.). So, again, when the Jewish forefathers called themselves " strangers and pilgrims upon earth " (Genesis xxiii. 4 ; xxviii. 4), the New Testament explains that this was their confession of faith in an invisible city having foundations, whose builder and maker was God (Hebrews xi. 9, 13).

And where our doctrine is patent, the meaning is often abundantly larger and more Divine than appears on the surface. It is a favourite canon of the sceptical and quasi-scientific criticism, that the value of a Scripture text equals the thought of the writer, never transcends it. What the writer intended to say—that is the thing said. And, no doubt, this canon is generally sound where history and matter of fact are concerned. But it is not sound—so far from this, it is the express contradiction of the principle laid down in the New Testament for our guidance in determining the meaning of doctrinal, prophetic, and spiritual texts. St. Peter's teaching is perfectly clear : the prophets did not comprehend the full significance of their own utterances— so far they were the passive organs of the Holy Ghost; they wrote with the knowledge that what they wrote had a hidden sense, which would only reveal itself, under supernatural illumination, to after-ages (1 Peter i. 10—12). And the entire treatment of the Old Testament by Christ and His Apostles argues, that where Divine truth is concerned, the interpreter must not be bound by the supposed conceptions of the writer, but is at liberty, within the limits drawn by the Bible Revelation as a whole—for we advocate no arbitrary, wild, and fatuous mode of exegesis— to hear the voice of the Spirit behind the letter, and to expound accordingly. And thus, when the earlier Volume of Scripture speaks of " salvation," and " life," and the righteous man's "hope," and the final " peace " and " rest " of those who serve God, we violate the very genius of the documents, if we do not, in a multitude of instances, take the texts with a length, and breadth, and depth, and height stretching immeasurably further than the poor ideas, which, at best, the authors must have had of the realities they wrote of. Viewed, indeed, in the glass of our principle, the Old Testament must be held to contain the seed of all which we now recognize as the Christian Doctrine of the Life to Come ; and with the New Testament in our hands, it is permitted to us—nay, it may even be a peremptory duty —to read this doctrine back into the earlier records of Inspiration, and so approximately to fix and determine their meaning in particular passages. In other words, it is competent to devout and thoughtful readers of the Old Testament, subject to the law of limitation just defined, to give a New Testament expansion and heightening to the terminology and language of the Old in treating of our subject.

At the same time, it was not reserved to the age of the Gospel to discover in the Old Testament a doctrine of the Future Life exceeding the literalities of the text. What is commonly regarded by the humanistic criticism as the mere theological development of the doctrine in Ezekiel, Daniel, and other later books of the canon, is often nothing more than the testimony of the earlier ones, reproduced with enlargement and commentary under the hand of the Illuminating Spirit. To the same origin may be safely attributed some, at least, of those remarkable aspects of our doctrine, which present themselves in the Apocrypha, in the older Rabbinism, in the dogmatic system of the Pharisees, Essenes, and other Jewish sects, and in the popular belief of Israel through the period of its national debasement and decay. In fact, the combined result of the standing instruction of the Sacred Text on the one hand, and of the evergrowing exposition furnished by Providence and the Inspiring Spirit on the other, appears to have been the formation in the end of a corpus of dogma relating to the Future Life, not without the seal of Divine authentication upon it, extending in various directions beyond the area of the written word, and not seldom running hard upon the ampler borders of the Gospel Revelation. How richly the doctrinal seed contained in Hebrew Scripture shot forth and blossomed just before Christ's advent, the celestial psalmody of Zachariah, Elizabeth, and Mary, the prophetic voices of Simeon and Anna, and the burning sermons of the Preacher of the Wilderness sufficiently testify. Who can doubt, indeed, that, all down the ages, from Moses to Christ, by the will of Him who indited the Bible, the knowledge of the Unseen State, conveyed by the letter, was, from time to time, indefinitely heightened to the minds of devout and lowly readers; and that unhistoric Simeons and Maries, not a few, waiting day and night for the kingdom of God, became possessors beforehand of treasures of wisdom and understanding; such as, in this lofty sphere, were otherwise the privileged reversion of the Church of Christ?

Still, for the most part, even the midday of Old Testament Saints was comparative darkness. The future of their contemplation was dull and hazy. At best they desired a clarity of knowledge, which the will of God denied to them. Life and immortality were brought to light by the Gospel. Christ was the discoverer of eternity. His appearance on earth gave mankind new proofs of the existence of it; and by His works and preaching He caused the whole realm of the unseen to blaze up into an unprecedented glory of reality, distinctness, and awful or transporting grandeur. Himself that Eternal Life which was in the beginning with the Father; the fountain of life to all being; He was found in fashion as a man, that mankind "might have life, and have it more abundantly." Atoning for sin by the blood of His cross, He disannulled death, and became "the author of eternal salvation to all them that obey Him." He died and was buried—yet saw no corruption. How should the cords of death bind down the Prince of Life? He rose from the dead and revived, according to the Scriptures. Nor this alone. Because obedient unto death, God also highly exalted Him, and caused Him to sit, in glorified humanity, at His own right hand in the heavens. There, as lord of lords, He administers the government of the universe; and there, as the high priest of the church, He intercedes and blesses. His Spirit draws all men to the Father, and gives supernatural knowledge of forgiveness of sins to all who believe. Angels are His servants, sent forth, as He ordains, to minister for the human heirs of salvation. The conflict of His people is with principalities, powers, and spiritual wickedness in high places—all these being ruled by man's ancient adversary, the Devil, who goes about as a destroyer. Meanwhile Christ, from His mediatorial throne, controls the might of this Spirit of Evil, and baffles His enterprises. He endues His servants with power from on high; and they overcome the world. Believers in Him do not perish. He has the keys of the Invisible State and of death, opening and no man shutting, shutting and no man opening. He is the Lord of the dead and the living. The wicked die. They go to the place of torment, and are punished in the presence of God and of the holy angels. The good die. Their bodies rest in the dust : they themselves are with Christ in paradise. So, on the one side or the other of a great gulf, which, in the unseen world, parts the disembodied spirits of men, the holy and unholy alike remain until Christ's foes are made His footstool. Then the voice of the archangel and the trump of God will usher in the great day of the Almighty, and, with it, the restitution of all things. The long absent Christ shall return in the clouds of heaven. The tenants of the graves, at His call, shall come forth and shall give public account before Him of the deeds done in the body. The wicked shall go away into everlasting fire, prepared for the Devil and his angels. Earth, the polluted theatre and platform of human iniquity, shall be burned up with a flame, causing the very heaven above it to shrivel like a parchment scroll. God shall create new heavens and a new earth, the inviolable and all-blessed home of righteousness. There, washed from their sins in the blood of the Lamb, the redeemed from among men shall live for ever in purity and bliss, inhabitants of God's holy city, worshippers in God's holy temple, joint-heirs with God's Eternal Son in the glory which He had with the Father before the world was. This is in outline the Gospel doctrine of the Unseen and Future Life ; and filled up as our knowledge and faith are able to fill it up, we see to how great a height it towers above all that can ever have been known by those who lived before the daybreak. They had the truth in rudiment. It is ours in its ripe growth and fruitfulness. They surveyed it in the mirror, and it was wondrous in their eyes. We see it face to face, and there is no veil between. They could never wholly disengage themselves from the chills of the grave and the gloom of Sheol. We, the disciples of Him of the open sepulchre, share His triumph over the power of darkness; and in prospect of our own mortal dissolution take up our parable—a parable which yet is not a parable—and say: "The sting of death is sin, and the strength of sin is the law: but thanks be unto God, which giveth us the victory through our Lord Jesus Christ!" Blessed indeed—as the Master told us—are our eyes which see and our ears which hear! And, if we know it, not the least part of our blessedness is, that, with the candle of the New Testament in our hands, God gives it to us, to see how in the Old He spoke mysteries of truth and grace to men from the beginning; to translate with adoring wonder and gladness the Divine symbols and hieroglyphs of Ancient Scripture into the dialect of Christian faith and anticipation; and to find in the mutual relations subsisting between the two great sections of the Holy Book impressive confirmation of St. Paul's sublime apostrophe:—"O the depth of the riches both of the wisdom and knowledge of God! how unsearchable are His judgments, and His ways past finding out! For who hath known the mind of the Lord? or who hath been His counsellor? . . . For of Him, and through Him, and to Him, are all things: to whom be glory for ever. Amen."

LONDON : R. NEEDHAM, PRINTER, PATERNOSTER-ROW.

www.ingramcontent.com/pod-product-compliance
Lightning Source LLC
Chambersburg PA
CBHW021519090426
42739CB00007B/690